Santa's Favorite Fishing Jokes

by Santa Claus
and His Helpers:

Russ Edwards and Jack Kreismer

Editorial: Ellen Fischbein

Artwork: Jack Kreismer Sr.

Contributor: Angela Demers

Cover and Page Design:
Fred and Diane Swartz

RED-LETTER PRESS, INC.
Saddle River, New Jersey

INTRODUCTION

One thing you can say about anyone who fishes...they'd better have a sense of humor. That's why, when anglers find Santa's Favorite Fishing Jokes *in their Christmas stocking or hip waders, they'll really be hooked.*

Filled with fish stories and tales out of school, this collection is far more than just a piscene fancy.

Just the thing for the old fishing Ho-Ho-Hole, Santa's Favorite Fishing Jokes *is the limit! Those who fish will never be up the creek for laughs as they trade the barbs, lines and biting jokes they caught in this book.*

Whether the Yuletide is high or low, smiles are always in season so, should you be thinking about the fishing pole or the North Pole, let Santa's Favorite Fishing Jokes *tackle your funny bone.*

𝕊anta Claus

P.S. Have a whale of a Christmas!

A FISHERMAN'S PRAYER

God grant that I may live to fish until my dying day

And when the final cast is made

And life has slipped away,

I pray that God's great landing net

Will catch me in its sweep

And in His mercy, God will judge me

Big enough to keep.

Two Texans went on an ice-fishing expedition in Minnesota. They gave up after only one day and returned home. When they were asked why they had come home so soon one of them replied, "Heck, it took us six hours just to get the boat in the water!"

Q: What's the best place to see a man-eating fish?

A: At a seafood restaurant

Charlie Brown tells us that happiness is a warm puppy. To this reporter, happiness is a cold trout.

—Eric Sevareid

*My luck! When the fish don't bite the
mosquitoes do.*
                              —Henny Youngman

The fisherman was arrested and brought to court for having caught fourteen more striped bass than the law allowed.

The judge asked, "How do you plead?"

"Guilty, your Honor," was the reply.

"That'll be 75 dollars plus costs," said the judge.

The fisherman paid the fine, then inquired of the judge, "Your Honor, if you don't mind, would it be possible to make some copies of the court record to take home to show my buddies?"

Warden: You're not allowed to fish here!

Fisherman: I'm not. I'm just teaching my worm how to swim.

At Sunday school, the teacher was leading the class in a discussion of what Noah might have done to pass time on the Ark.

"I think he went fishing," said one little girl.

The little boy sitting beside her gave her a look and piped up, "What...with only two worms?!?"

There is a peculiar pleasure in catching trout in a place where nobody thinks of looking for them, and at an hour when everybody believes they cannot be caught.

—Henry Van Dyke

Fishing seems to be the favorite form of loafing.

—Ed Howe

The ladies at the coffee klatch were all admiring a huge stuffed shark which was mounted over Mabel's mantelpiece above the fireplace. Mabel grinned proudly and said, "My husband and I landed that one on a deep-sea fishing trip."

"What is it stuffed with?" asked one of the women.

"My husband."

A guy was telling his co-workers about his fishing trip. "You should have seen the big one that got away," he said.

"Yeah, I'll bet it was as big as a whale," his boss chided.

"A whale? I was using a whale for bait!"

T he answer is net profit. And the question?

What does a fisherman earn?

If you can keep your hands in your pockets and make a convincing talk about the fish that got away, you can be a successful salesman.

                —Anonymous

You might be a redneck if you've been too drunk to fish.

—Jeff Foxworthy

Bank customer: I need a thousand dollar loan to go on a fishing trip.

Loan officer: That might be arranged, but we need collateral. Do you own a car?

Bank customer: Oh, certainly. I have several...a Porsche, a Jaguar and a Rolls Royce.

Loan officer: How about a boat?

Bank customer: Sure do. As a matter of fact, I'm taking my yacht on the fishing trip.

Loan officer: And a house?

Bank customer: Oh yes. I have a townhouse and an estate in the country as well as a couple of condos in Florida.

Loan officer: Oh, come on! You must be joking!

Bank customer: Well, you started it!

I have good news and bad news about your movie script," said the agent to the author of *Fish Tales*.

"What's the good news?" asked the author.

"Spielberg loved your script...He just ate it up."

"And the bad news?"

"Spielberg's my dog."

Getting the fish through customs will be easy. The hard part is getting them to sit still for their visa pictures.

—Goodwill Games official Bob Walsh,
on shipping Washington state trout
to Moscow

The fishing was so bad that even the liars didn't catch any.

—Sanford Mims

A guy goes into a sporting goods store.

"Remember all that expensive fishing equipment you sold me a few weeks ago?"

"I certainly do."

"Remember that you told me it was well worth the expense because of all the fish I'd be catching?"

"Yep."

"Well, would you mind telling me again? I'm getting a bit discouraged."

Digby went over to Carlton's house where he found his friend fishing in the basement.

"What the heck are you doing?" asked Digby.

"I got fed up with pumping it out all the time," responded Carlton, "so now I've had it stocked."

HO-HO-HO!

Jingles, Santa's right-hand elf, can sometimes take things a bit too literally. One time he was going fishing and only put on one boot because he heard the stream was one foot above normal.

Fishing is an employment for my idle time, which is then not idly spent.

—Henry Wotton

Fishing is the art of the wrist with a twist.

—Roy Van Horn

A banker went fishing with one of his customers. They were out on a boat in the river when the vessel smashed into a rock and tipped over, spilling the guys into the drink. The customer noticed the banker flailing away and said, "Say, can you float alone?"

"Oh, c'mon!" exclaimed the banker. "I'm drowning and you want to talk business!?!"

In Miami, a fisherman ran into a dockside bar and said to the bartender, "Quick, give me a drink before the fight starts."

The bartender gave him a drink and he knocked it back and ran out the door.

A moment later, he ran back in and said, "Give me a drink before the fight starts."

Once again, he downed the booze and dashed out the door.

A minute later he was back again and said, "I need a drink before the fight starts."

The bartender slammed down the bottle and snapped, "Wait a minute! Who's going to pay for all these drinks?"

And the fisherman said, "Uh oh, the fight's about to start."

Fish may be bought if they can't be caught.

—Gene Demers

HO·HO·HO!

Mrs. Claus had been bugging Santa to take her along on one of his summer fishing trips and finally Santa agreed. They chartered a deep-sea fishing boat and headed out early in the morning for a day of shark fishing.

As Mrs. Claus had never been fishing, Santa had to show her all the ropes...or the lines, as it were.

He showed her how to bait the hook, cast and jiggle the bait in the water and then left her on the portside while he went over to starboard so as not to be disturbed.

It was quiet for about an hour when Mrs. Claus had a strike.

"Oh my heavens, Santa!" Mrs. Claus cried out. "I think it's a shark. It's got a big dorsal fin and lots of teeth!"

"How big is it?" asked Santa.

"It must be at least twelve inches!" Mrs. Claus exclaimed.

"Twelve inches," Santa snorted. "Ho-ho-ho...twelve inches is a baby—a new spawn—not worth the bait. That's tiny."

"Tiny?" Mrs. Claus called out. "That's twelve inches between the eyes!"

Waitee: Waiter, I don't like the looks of this bluefish.

Waiter: If you're interested in looks, you should have ordered goldfish.

Q: What's essential to have when ice fishing?

A: Good ice site

Nothing grows faster than a fish between the time the fish takes the bait...and the time he gets away.

—Tom Lehmann

George Washington couldn't have been a fisherman. He never told a lie.

—Jeffrey Kreismer

R iley and Baxter were out on the lake at the crack of dawn. They cast for trout, sat silently and kept still so they wouldn't frighten off the fish.

Five hours later, Baxter shifted his feet.

"What is it with you?" snapped Riley. "Make up your mind. Did you come here to fish or to dance?"

F isherman One: That's a beautiful rod you've got there.

Fisherman Two: Thanks. Actually, I got it for the wife.

Fisherman One: Nice trade.

Q: Why did the fisherman have "TGIF" on his hip waders?

A: As a reminder that "Toes Go In First"

Then there was the fisherman who observed a bunch of ostriches along the shoreline. It seems they were about to throw a surprise party to honor one of their own. At the appointed time the ostrich of honor was spotted heading toward them.

"Here he comes!" the lookout ostrich whispered. "Quick, everybody. Get your heads in the sand!"

A fish probably goes home and lies about the bait he stole.

—Roy Harry

FISHERMAN'S HOROSCOPE

Aquarius (Jan 20-Feb 18) The Tackle Box
Born under the sign of the Water Carrier, you are
still patiently waiting for your ship to come in.
Have you noticed, though, that the tide is getting
up over your hip waders?

Pisces (Feb 19-Mar 20) The Fish
It's ironic that you are a Pisces as you have
utterly no natural ability as an angler. In fact,
what you do can't properly be termed "fishing";
it's more like you're just drowning worms.

Aries (Mar 21-Apr 19) The Net
As an Aries, your goal today should be nothing
less than peace, tranquility and oneness with the
universe. If you can't swing that, fishing and a
brew sound good.

Taurus (Apr 20-May 20) The Fish Story
Born with determination and the love of the chase,
you are what they call a "sport fisherman"...as
opposed to one who actually catches something.

Gemini (May 21-Jun 21) The Fishing Pole
With Gemini ruling your life, you are well aware of
the duality of existence. You'd do well to remember
that there's a fine line between fishing and just
standing on the shore looking like a dope.

Cancer (Jun 22-Jul 22) The Crab Trap
Being born under the sign of the Crab bodes ill
for your domestic life. Your wife will confront you
by asking which is more important—fishing or her?
The real trouble will come when you respond,
 "Deep sea or freshwater?"

Leo (Jul 23-Aug 22) The Line
Soon, while fishing in the ocean, you'll be overcome with the certainty that all your troubles are behind you. This revelation will come as a moray eel bites through the seat of your pants.

Virgo (Aug 23-Sep 22) The Lure
You have mastered the art of thinking like a fish. In fact, you're apt to fall for anything...hook, line and sinker.

Libra (Sep 23-Oct 23) The Fish Scales
Both in your daily life and in fishing, your life has served as a beacon to others—much like a lighthouse warning people off the rocks.

Scorpio (Oct 24-Nov 21) The Bait
You are an avid fisherman who spends every spare moment and your last dollar on your passion. This explains why all other aspects of your life are pretty much "up the creek."

Sagittarius (Nov 22-Dec 21) The Hook
Born under the influence of this sign, your delusions of fishing are doomed to failure. You couldn't catch a fish if it were coated in batter and swimming in tartar sauce.

Capricorn (Dec 22-Jan 19) The Boot
The stars predict that you will soon sign a multi-million dollar endorsement contract for the world's leading rod and reel manufacturer. Now your only problem will be getting them to sign it!

There are sport fishermen, and then there are those who catch fish!

—Milton Berle

Q: What do you say to a guy when his lure is in the seaweed?

A: Your fly is down.

Little Johnny's teacher asked him to give the class an example of the line of least resistance.

"No problem," said Johnny. "That would be a fishing line with no bait on it."

A duck walks into a convenience store and asks, "Do you sell any bait here?"

The manager says, "No, we don't carry bait."

The next day the duck walks into the store and asks, "Do you sell any bait?"

The manager says, "No, we don't have bait here."

The third day the duck walks into the store and asks, "Do you have any bait?"

The manager says, "Look! If I told you once, I told you three times, we don't have any bait here! The next time you come in here asking for bait, I'm gonna nail your webbed feet to the wall!"

The next day the duck enters the store and asks, "Do you have any nails?"

The manager says, "No. We don't sell nails here."

The duck says, "Good. Do you have any bait?"

So frequent the casts. So seldom a strike.

—Arnold Gingrich

*Every man in his life has a fish that
haunts him.*

—Negley Farson

Q: What happened when the captain of the river
fishing boat peeled onions?

A: It made the Bridge on the River Kwai.

Then there was the guy who was duped into
buying a piece of land that turned out to be
under water. When he went back to complain, the
salesman sold him a boat and a fishing pole.

Maggie: I thought I saw your husband fishing down at the lake.

Aggie: Did he catch anything?

Maggie: It looked like he caught a few.

Aggie: Then it couldn't have been my husband.

Q: How do baby fish swim?

A: Roe after roe

The two best times to go fishing are when it's raining and when it's not.

—Fishing Proverb

*If people concentrated on the really
important things in life, there'd be a
shortage of fishing poles.*

—Doug Larson

Pupils at an elementary school were asked to write in 50 words or less the effect of oil on fish.

An eleven-year-old wrote, "Last night my mother opened a can of sardines. It was full of oil and all the fish were dead."

Q: What's the difference between a hunter and a fisherman?

A: A hunter lies in wait and a fisherman waits and lies.

On the trail down to the old fishin' hole, a small boy with a fishing pole in hand ran past an old man.

The old man was amused and called after the little boy, "Goin' fishing, sonny?"

The little boy called back, "Sure am."

"Got worms?" asked the old codger with a smile.

"Yep," the boy answered. "But I'm going fishin' anyway."

I don't want to sit at the head table anymore. I want to go fishing.

—President George Bush

*Fishing is not a matter of life and death. It
is much more important than that.*

—Jim Tomlinson

An avid angler on a fishing trip was at it for
almost two weeks before he caught his first
fish. When he got back to his hotel, he faxed his
wife: "I've got one. She's a real beauty...weighs
seven pounds. I'll be home in a couple of days."

His wife responded with this fax: "I've got one as
well. She also weighs seven pounds and is a real
beauty, too. Come home at once."

Bob: How big was that fish you caught?

Rob: It was so big, the photograph weighed five
pounds.

A guy is eating a bald eagle and gets caught by the game warden. He's brought to trial for killing an endangered species. The judge says, "Are you aware that eating a bald eagle is a federal offense?"

The guy answers, "Yes, but I have an explanation...I got lost in the woods and didn't have anything to eat for two weeks. I saw this bald eagle swooping down for fish at the lake. I figured I might be able to steal some fish as the eagle grabbed them. Unfortunately, when I went to grab for the fish, my fist hit the eagle in the head and killed 'im. I reckoned that, since the eagle was dead, I might as well eat it since it would be a waste to just let it rot."

After a brief recess, the judge comes back with his ruling.

"Due to the extreme conditions you endured, added to the fact that the bald eagle's death was accidental rather than intentional, I find you not guilty."

As an aside, the judge asks the guy, "By the way, what does a bald eagle taste like?"

The guy responds, "The best way to describe it is that it tastes like a cross between an owl and an egret."

De-fin-itions

Live bait: the biggest fish you got to handle all day

Thumb: a temporary hook holder

Fisherman: a jerk at one end of the line waiting for a jerk at the other end

Sinker: a weight hopefully big enough to knock out any fish on the way to the bottom so that it floats to the surface

Rookie angler: the one who catches the most and biggest fish

Fishing rod: a stick with a worm on one end and a fool at the other

Truth: when one fisherman calls another fisherman a liar

Two old codgers were reminiscing as they sat at the end of the pier with their lines in the water.

"My first girlfriend was Mary Katherine Agnes Colleen Patricia Marion Margaret Kathleen O'Shaugnessy. I carved her name in a piling."

"Whatever happened?" asked his friend.

"The pier collapsed."

Q: What do you get when you cross a piranha with a petunia?

A: I don't know but I wouldn't try smelling it.

A fish story backed by visual evidence is something you don't run into every day.

—Red Smith

"Angling" is the name given to fishing by people who can't fish.

—Stephen Leacock

Did you hear the one about the fishing trawler that collided with the tanker carrying red and brown paint?

The crew was marooned.

Farnsworth, affectionately known as the "fishing fibber" for tales about "the big one that got away", was terribly ill. His wife, visiting him in the hospital, asked the doctor how he was doing. The doctor responded, "I'm afraid he's lying at death's door."

"Imagine that," said the wife. "He's about to meet his maker and he's still lying."

HO-HO-HO!

Q: What's the meanest fish in the Arctic Ocean?

A: Santa Jaws

The answer is The Congressional Herring.
And the question?

What's the most powerful fish in Washington, D.C.?

Fishing is the eternal fountain of youth.
There is said to be a tablet of 2000 B.C.
which says: 'Gods do not subtract from
the allotted span of men's lives the hours
spent fishing.'

—President Herbert Hoover

There is no use in walking five miles to fish when you can depend on being just as unsuccessful near home.

—Mark Twain

A guy knocks on Dooley's door. When Mrs. Dooley answers it the guy says, "Hi. I'm looking for Mr. Dooley."

"He's not here," says Mrs. Dooley. "Can I help you?"

"I'm afraid not. I wanted to talk to him about our Fishing Association meeting. Do you know where I can find him?"

"Yeah...just head down to the river and look for a stick with a worm on both ends."

HO·HO·HO!

Sometimes I think my elves don't get out enough. Last summer Elfis and Ollie went fishing in Vermont and they had a pretty good day, each catching their limit.

As they returned to the dock Elfis said to Ollie, "I hope you remembered the spot where we caught all the fish."

"Sure did," replied Ollie. "I put a big 'X' on the side of the boat to mark the spot."

"Phooey...that's not going to work!" snorted Elfis. "How do you know we'll get the same boat tomorrow?"

There ain't but one time to go fishin', and that's whenever you can.

—Diron Talbert

A wheeler-dealer entrepreneur was on vacation at the beach when he noticed what appeared to be a lazy fisherman sitting leisurely by the water with his pole propped up in the sand and his line cast out into the water.

"Hey, bud," said the entrepreneur. "You're not going to catch any fish that way. You should be at work, anyway."

The fisherman responded, "Oh yeah? Why should I be at work?"

"Because you'll make money and then you can buy a boat which will enable you to catch more fish," said the entrepreneur.

"Why do you think that would be good for me?" questioned the fisherman.

The entrepreneur was becoming a bit irritated answering the fisherman's questions.

"That would be good for you because you'd eventually be able to buy a bigger boat and hire other fishermen to work for you," he said.

"Why is that so good for me?" asked the fisherman.

Now the entrepreneur was highly agitated. "Look...you don't seem to get the point. When all is said and done, you could wind up with a whole fleet of fishing boats and amass great fortunes."

"And then what would happen?" asked the fisherman.

The entrepreneur, steaming mad, barked, "What would happen?!? You'd become filthy rich and would never have to work again! You could spend the rest of your years sitting on this beach fishing without a care in the world."

The fisherman smiled at the entrepreneur and said, "And what do you think I'm doing right now?"

I went fishing with a dotted line and caught every other fish.

—Steven Wright

Your typical fisherman is long on optimism and short on memory.

—Ken Polish

Then there was the fisherman who produced an excellent movie...mainly because he had a great cast.

A guy goes to a doctor for a physical. Afterwards the doctor says, "I've got some good news and bad news."

The guy says, "Give me the bad news first."

The doctor says, "You've got a disease that we don't know how to treat."

"Oh my gosh! What could possibly be the good news?"

"I caught an eight pound bass yesterday."

Q: What did one sardine say to the other sardine when it saw a submarine?

A: Look! There goes a can full of people.

A businesswoman vacationing in Boca Raton is strolling along the beach when she runs into a fisherman who, with his line in the water, is patiently waiting for a bite. The fisherman likes what he sees and says, "Hey, hon, would you like a little company?"

She replies, "Do you have one to sell?"

It really is true that when some fishermen tell a tale, they will go to any length.

—Tom Tucci

Fishermen don't lie. They just tell beautiful stories.

—Syngman Rhee

The fisherman had a shopping cart full of angling equipment as he made his way to the cash register. Watching the cashier ring up hundreds of dollars worth of gear, he sighed, "You know, if you'd start selling fish here, you could save me a bundle of money."

Maybe you've heard about the new glass-bottomed boats. Now the fish can boast about how big the guy was they got away from.

Waldo: My wife and me had another argument about me fishin' all the time.

Vinnie: Oh yeah? How'd it turn out?

Waldo: The usual. She came crawling to me on her hands and knees.

Vinnie: Really? What'd she say?

Waldo: She said, "Come out from under that bed, you miserable weasel, and fight like a man!"

Q: Why can't bad actors fish?

A: They never remember their lines.

Fishing is a stick and a string with a fly on one end and a fool at the other.

—Ed O'Brien

I never lost a little fish—yes,

I am free to say

It always was the biggest fish I caught

that got away.

—Eugene Field

When fish eat, why don't they have to wait an hour before going swimming?

A girl went fishing for the first time with her boyfriend. As they sat in their rowboat on the lake, she asked, "How much was that red and white thing?"

"Oh, you mean the float? That's only about a nickel."

"I guess I owe you a nickel then. My float just sank."

A guy saw a fisherman catch a giant trout only to throw it back into the water. A few minutes later, he nabbed another huge trout but tossed that away, too. Then he caught a little trout, smiled and put it into his cooler for safekeeping.

The guy who was watching the fisherman asked, "How come you threw away the big fish and kept the small one?"

The fisherman replied, "Small frying pan."

Moby: I was just about to nab a whale of a fish when my line snapped.

Dick: What a reel disappointment!

The best thing about fishing is that it gives you something to do while you're doing nothing.

—Gary Greer

Santa's Top Ten Groaners

1. What do fish get if they don't like the bait that fishermen are using?

    A re-bait

2. How do you manage to keep a killer fish behind bars?

    Strong lox

3. What do sea monsters eat?

    Fish and ships

4. What is a frog's favorite sport?

    Fly fishing

5. What did the angler take home from the baseball game?

    The catch of the day

6. Where did the fish go to get its nose fixed?

   To the plastic sturgeon

7. Why couldn't Batman go fishing?

   Because Robin ate all the worms

8. What do Texans call sushi?

   Bait

9. What fish was a famous actress?

   Marlin Monroe

10. Where do ghosts fish in North America?

    Lake Eerie

Bragging may not bring happiness, but no man having caught a large fish goes home through an alley.

—Anonymous

Why is it that fish always seem to go on vacation at the same time we do?

—Bob Matistic

Three old geezers were sitting on a bench in New York City's Central Park. The one in the middle was reading a newspaper while the other two were pretending to fish. A policeman on the beat watched them as they baited imaginary hooks, cast their lines and reeled in their fake catches.

"Do you know these two?" the cop asked the guy reading the paper.

"Sure. They're buddies of mine."

"Well, they're disturbin' the other people. You better get them outta here!"

"Yes, officer," said the guy, and with that he furiously began rowing.

A fisherman dies and goes to Hell. He can't believe it when the devil gives him a tour and shows him a fishing hole loaded with giant fish...you name it—salmon, bass, trout—the works. The devil hands the guy a fishing pole.

"Wow, this is great!" exclaims the guy. "Where can I get some bait?"

"Nowhere," says the devil. "That's the hell of it."

"So, Eddie, what did Daddy say when his line broke and the big fish got away?"

"Should I leave out the swear words, Mom?"

"Please do."

"He didn't say anything."

How far a fisherman will stretch the truth is a matter of the length of his arms.

—Genevieve Johnson

I used to go fishing until it struck me...

You can buy fish. What the hell am I doing

in a boat at four-thirty in the morning?

If I want a hamburger, I don't track cattle

down.

—Kenny Potchenson

Sportsman #1: Have you ever hunted bear?

Sportsman #2: No, but I've gone fishing in my shorts.

Maybe you've heard the one about the fisherman who caught a 220 pound tuna, but had to throw it back. It was a piano tuner.

Co-workers are talking Monday morning. One says to the other, "What did you do over the weekend?"

The other succinctly says, "Dropped hooks into the water."

The first one says, "So you went fishing, eh?"

"No, golfing."

Bathroom Graffiti: Mrs. Paul's Fish Sticks. Does Yours?

Fishing is a delusion entirely surrounded by liars in old clothes.

—Don Marquis

Charlie's new job as a commercial fisherman promised to have him spending a lot of time at sea. Concerned for his wife's security for those times he'd be fishing the hours away, he decided to stop at a pet shop to look at watchdogs.

When the pet shop owner showed him a French poodle Charlie smirked, "C'mon, that dog couldn't hurt a flea."

"Ah, but you don't understand," said the pet shop owner. "This dog knows karate."

With that, the pet shop owner pointed to a two-by-four and commanded, "Karate the wood!"

The litttle dog split it in half. The pet shop owner then pointed to a thick telephone directory and instructed, "Karate the telephone book!"

Again, the dog split the book in two. Charlie was convinced. He bought the dog.

He brought the dog home and explained to his wife that he'd purchased a watchdog for her.

When she saw the tiny French poodle she scoffed, "That little thing. You've got to be kidding."

Charlie remarked, "But this poodle is incredible. He's a karate expert."

"Yeah, right," Charlie's wife said. "Karate my foot."

Clem and Jethro are standing in the creek fishing on a quiet Sunday afternoon.

Clem: Did I tell you the new one I heard the other day?

Jethro: Was it funny?

Clem: Yeah.

Jethro: Then you haven't told me.

Q: What do fighters and fishermen have in common?

A: Both attempt to land a hook in the jaw.

A golfer has one advantage over the fisherman...He doesn't have to show anything to prove his success.

—Anonymous

Fishing Lines
Santa's Favorite One-Liners

There are two periods when fishing is good...before you get there and after you leave.

A fisherman is a man who baits and sees.

Nothing makes a fish bigger than almost being caught.

A fisherman is a guy who catches a big fish by patience, and sometimes by luck, but most often by the tale.

Old fishermen never die...They just smell that way.

A fish wouldn't get caught if it kept its mouth shut.

A guy will sit on a boat all day hoping to catch a fish, then won't hesitate to complain if his dinner is a few minutes late.

In a world without fish there would be a lot less lying.

Nothing grows faster than a fish from the time he bites until the time he gets away.

A fisherman is a man who spends rainy days sitting around on the muddy banks of rivers doing nothing because his wife won't let him do it at home.

An optimist is a fisherman who brings along a camera.

An angler is one who, first, lies in wait for a fish and then lies in weight after he lands it.

To catch a fish you have to worm your way into its confidence.

Don't hurry...Settle back...Then bait and see.
                              —Fishing Proverb

A couple of Eskimos went fishing on an extremely frigid day. They lit a fire in the bottom of their kayak to warm up but moments later the blaze raged out of control and their boat sank.

The moral of the story: You can't have your kayak and heat it, too.

Q: What do you get if you cross a fish with an elephant?

A: Swimming trunks

Harry: How are you supposed to fish on a frozen lake?

Larry: Well, what I do is cut a hole in the ice and then I hold my wrist watch over it. When a fish comes up to see what time it is, that's when I net him.

Did you hear the one about the new horror movie where they cross a killer shark with Nessie, Scotland's most famous monster? It's called Loch Jaws.

Suckers are trash fish, an insult to divinity. They have chubby, humanoid lips and appear to be begging for cigars.

—Bill Barich

*Good fishing is nothing more than a
matter of timing. You have to get there
yesterday.*

—Steve Freebairn

The clergyman bumped into one of the church members at a local outing one Sunday afternoon.

"So I heard you played golf instead of coming to church this morning, eh Bagsby?"

"Not so," said Bagsby. "And I've got the fish to prove it."

Q: What fish is famous?

A: Starfish

A couple of guys were fishing on the lake when one them says to the other, "You know, I had this dream last night where I was on a fishing trip and the bass were biting like crazy. No sooner would I get my line in the water, when I'd land one after the other."

"Wow! I had a great dream, too," replies the second angler. "I dreamed I had a date with Cindy Crawford and Sharon Stone."

"What? You dreamed you had a date with two girls and you didn't call me?"

"I did, but your roommate said you were on a fishing trip."

To live is not necessary.

To fish is necessary.

—Latin Proverb

'Lord, suffer me to catch a fish so large

that even I in talking of it afterward shall

have no need to lie.'

—Suggested motto for President Herbert
Hoover's fishing lodge

Game Warden: Hey...you need a permit to fish here!

Fishin' Fred: Why? So far I've been doing pretty good with just worms.

Pelican one: Pretty good fish you have there.

Pelican two: Well, it fills the bill.

"Just how credible is this witness?" asked the judge of the attorney who wanted to call someone to the stand.

"Your Honor, I've known him to go fishing all day and admit that he didn't have a single bite."

Q: How are a priest and a fisherman who throws back all of his catches alike?

A: They both try to save soles.

If a man fishes hard, what is he going to do easy?

—Roy Blount, Jr.

When you fall in a river, you're no longer a fisherman; you're a swimmer.

—Gene Hill

One day at the fishing hole, an elephant happened to notice a snapping turtle sunning itself on a rock.

Without provocation, the elephant went over to the snapper, picked it up with his trunk and threw it through the air over the trees.

A fisherman with his line in the water nearby, said, "Hey, why'd you do that? That turtle was minding its own business."

"Well," replied the elephant, "I was drinking water and I happened to remember that same snapper took a chunk out of my trunk twenty years ago."

"Man! What a memory!" exclaimed the fisherman.

"All elephants have it," responded the pachyderm modestly. "It's called turtle recall."

A fishing boat goes down with only one man surviving and he's washed ashore on a remote island inhabited by cannibals. They capture him and tie him to a stake where they proceed to nick him with their spears and drink his blood. This goes on for two weeks. The guy can't take it any longer and asks to see the chief. When the cannibal leader arrives the guy says, "Look, chief...either let me go or kill me. I'm tired of being stuck for the drinks."

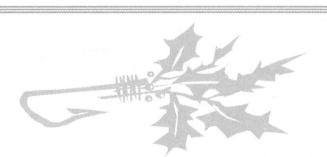

A trout is a fish known mainly by hearsay. It lives on anything not included in a fisherman's equipment.

—H.I. Phillips

You can always tell a fisherman, but you can't tell him much.

—Corey Ford

Fisherman: Father, is it a sin to fish on Sunday?

Priest: From what I understand about the few fish you catch, it's a sin any day you fish.

A guy's terribly sick on the ocean fishing trip. Unaware of this, the captain's mate comes up to him and inquires, "We have complimentary sandwiches on board. Can I bring you one?"

The guy answers, "Naah...just throw it overboard and save me the trouble."

There was a sign on a bait and tackle shop which read, "Fishing Tickle."

A customer walked in, told the owner of the spelling error and then asked, "How long has that sign been like that?"

"Oh, for many years," replied the owner.

"Hasn't anyone else told you of the error?" questioned the customer.

"Oh sure. That's how I get customers."

A woman without a man is like a fish without a bicycle.

—Attributed to Gloria Steinem

There's nothing a fisherman can do if his worm ain't trying!

—Anonymous

A clergymen saw a young boy fishing at the local lake. Realizing the kid hadn't been to church that Sunday morning, he asked the boy, "Young man, do you know the parables?"

"Of course," was the response.

"Well then, which one do you find the most inspiring?"

"The one where everybody loafs and fishes."

The answer is bassinet. And the question?

What makes fishermen happy?

The wife is telling her friend about her recent vacation to Venice, Italy.

The friend asks, "What did your husband like best about it...the art, the statues or the architecture?"

"Oh, none of those things. His favorite was being able to sit in the hotel and fish from the window."

Any man who pits his intelligence against a fish and loses has it coming.

—John Steinbeck

Bumper Snickers

FISHERMEN GET THE BLUES

WOMEN WANT ME, FISH FEAR ME

WHEN FISHERMEN DRINK,
THEY ASSIGN A DESIGNATED DIVER

FISH STORIES TOLD HERE

GET REEL!

I FISH, THEREFORE I LIE

I CATCH FISH BY THE TALE

COMMUNICATE WITH A FISH—DROP HIM A LINE

OLD FISHERMEN NEVER DIE,
THEY JUST LOSE THEIR MUSSELS

A guy goes ice fishing in Minnesota for the first time. He's not having any luck at all but another guy sitting close by is pulling up fish left and right. The novice ice fisherman asks the guy, "What's the trick?"

The ice fisherman mumbles, "Mmumottameepdammrmsmmrm."

"What'd you say?"

"Mmumottameepdammrmsmmrm."

"I still don't understand you."

With that, the ice fisherman opens his thermos, spits into it a couple of times and then says, "I said you've got to keep the worms warm."

I would rather fish than eat, particularly eat fish.

—Corey Ford

The fish begged the man not to throw him back.

—Dick Cavett, speaking of an undersized
fish which was caught by an angler
on the polluted Hudson River

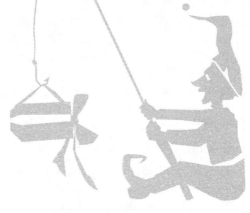

The local fishing club was having its annual
dinner with the usual ceremonies and trophy
presentations. One of the first-timers there noticed
that the chairs were spaced seven feet from each
other and asked one of the club's directors how
come they were so far apart.

"Oh, we always do that," said the director. "We
want to make sure that the members can do full
justice to their fish stories."

Q: What would you call the only fish that wasn't caught?

A: The sole survivor

Waiter: Can I help you sir?

Waitee: I've been waiting for my meal for the longest time.

Waiter: Your fish will be coming very soon, sir.

Waitee: Tell me. What kind of bait are you using?

No man has ever caught a fish as big as the one that got away.

—Remy Walsh

A woman who has never seen her husband fishing doesn't know what a patient man she has married.

—Ed Howe

A guy went on an ocean fishing expedition and fell overboard in shark-infested waters. The guy couldn't swim and screamed for help. A lawyer who happened to be on the trip dove in to save him. All of a sudden, sharks formed a two-lane convoy and escorted the lawyer and the guy he was dragging to shore. Safely ashore, the guy thanked the lawyer profusely but was extremely puzzled. "I don't understand it," he said. "Why did the sharks do that?"

"Simple," replied the lawyer. "Professional courtesy."

G us and Pete, two old fishing buddies, were comparing their exploits, each trying to outdo the other.

"Once, up in Newfoundland during a full North Atlantic gale, I caught a herring," Gus said. "And I'm tellin' you, Pete, it was the biggest herring that ever lived. It weighed at least 500 pounds!"

"That's nothing, Gus," retaliated Pete. "Down in the Keys, I pulled up my line and on the hook was a ship's lamp. On the bottom, there was the date 1392...a full century before Columbus! And get this...inside the lamp, the light was still burning!"

Gus studied his buddy's face for a few moments before cracking a smile. "Tell you what, Pete...let's compromise. I'll knock 475 pounds off the herring and you blow out the light!"

Fishing is an idle sport that makes men and truth strangers.

—Anonymous

Give me the patience to sit calmly by,

While amateurs with veterans gravel vie,

Recounting deeds performed with rod and fly.

Then help me tell the Final, Crowning Lie!

—C. J. Judd

Old Fisbin was leaning over the bar, crying in his beer.

"My wife says if I ever go fishin' again, she's going to leave me."

"Gee that's tough," his friend commiserated.

"Yeah," sniffed Fisbin, wiping a tear from his eye. "I'm sure going to miss her."

Barney: You've been watching me fish for two hours now. Why not try it yourself?

Arnie: I don't have the patience for it.

Q: What is it called when a group of atomic scientists goes out on a weekend angling trip?

A: Nuclear fishin'

Fish and visitors stink in three days.

—Benjamin Franklin

Give a man a fish and he eats for a day.
Teach him how to fish and you get rid of
him for the whole weekend.

—Zenna Schaffer

A fisherman was suing a shipping company. He was on the stand when his lawyer asked, "Would you please tell the court what happened when the ship filled with string crashed into your fishing boat?"

"Yes. I was stranded."

Smithers had a miserable time of it on the lake, not a single bite all day. On his way home, he stopped at the fish market and ordered catfish.

"Pick out four big ones and throw them at me," he told the fish monger.

"Why would you want me to throw them at you?"

"Because I want to be able to tell my wife that I caught them," replied Smithers.

"In that case I think you should take the salmon."

"Why's that?"

"Because your wife came in and said that if you stopped by, she'd prefer salmon for dinner tonight."

A bad day fishing still beats a good day working.

—Fishing Proverb

There's a fine line between fishing and just standing on the shore like an idiot.

—Steven Wright

The family was set to take off on vacation when the wife announces, "The car's packed, but now that we've got all your fishing tackle in it, there's no room for the kids."

The husband says, "Well, I hope you left enough food for them."

The answer is Three Men and a Baby. And the question?

What do you get when four men go fishing and one comes back without having a single catch?

The minister asked the boy why he was late for Sunday school.

"I wanted to go fishing but my dad wouldn't let me," said the boy.

"Well, you've got a good father there, son. And I'm sure he explained why you couldn't go fishing today, right?"

"Yes. He said there wasn't enough bait for two of us."

Many fishermen catch their fish by their tale.

—Kevin Schifftner

Rod & Rhyme

Early to bed
Early to rise
Fish all day
Make up lies.

A three pound pull, and a five-pound bite;
An eight-pound jump, and a ten-pound fight;
A twelve-pound bend to your pole—but alas!
When you get him aboard he's a half-pound bass!

An answer to this question
Is what I greatly wish;
Does fishing make men liars—
Or do only liars fish?

Old Noah went a-fishing;
He sat upon the ark
And kept his hooks a-dangle
From daybreak on to dark.
His catch was pretty meager,
But everyone affirms
He had not a chance, because he
Had just a pair of worms.

—St. Clair Adams

A guy is going on a fishing trip and promises his wife that he'll send her the first trout he catches. Four days later a UPS driver pulls up with a package for the guy's wife.

The wife looks at the package and says to the UPS driver, "My husband never does anything right. He said he'd send me a trout and look at this. It's marked COD."

I guess you can say we added some

Finns to the Sharks.

—Kevin Constantine, coach of the
National Hockey League's
San Jose Sharks, after drafting
five players from Finland

Religious freedom is the right to attend the church of your choice, or go fishing.

—Jay Kaye

HO-HO-HO!

"Mommy, tell me. Are you sure I'm a polar bear?" asked the little polar bear.

"Why of course you are, honey. You live right here at the North Pole just as Santa Claus does. You like to do fun things like chasing after seals in the snow. And you swim under the ice to catch fish. Of course you're a polar bear, but why do you ask?"

"Because I'm *freezing*!"

Q: What happened when the fishing boat sank in piranha fish-infested waters?

A: It came back with a skeleton crew.

A guy goes to the doctor for a thorough physical. Afterwards, the doctor informs him that he needs surgery.

The guy says, "Doc, I can't have surgery now. I'm going on a big fishing trip next week. Isn't there anything you can do?"

"Well, I suppose I could touch up the x-rays."

Buford: I went fishing yesterday and caught six blues, three trout, two bass and I also got a panfor.

Farnsworth: What's a panfor?

Buford: To cook 'em in.

I watched a fishing show today on television. Have you ever watched fishing for about fifteen minutes and said, "Boy, I need a life?"

—Brian Regan

Going to a fishing convention with your wife is like going fishing with the game warden.

—Joe Dolan

Ralph: You going to have your wife cook that fish for you?

Harry: No way. She's such a lousy cook you say grace after you eat!

Game Warden: Hey, don't you see that sign that says 'No Fishing'?

Fisherman: Sure do. The fella' that painted that sign sure knew what he was talkin' about.

A Minnesota fellow who had never been ice fishing decided that it was time to enjoy the experience so, over the Christmas holidays, he borrowed an auger and some tackle and headed out on the ice alone.

As he began augering the hole, a voice from above boomed, "There are no fish under the ice!"

The guy shook his head and smacked the side of his ear. He thought he must have been hearing things and returned to cutting the ice hole.

Again a voice boomed down, "There are no fish under the ice!"

Figuring that it must be the wind playing tricks on him, the novice ice fisherman ignored the voice and continued boring the hole.

One more time the voice rang out, "I told you...There are no fish under the ice!"

At that point, the fisherman looked up and said, "Who is this, God?"

The voice boomed down, "No, it's the arena manager."

If anglers talked only about the fish they really caught, the silence would be unbearable.

—Dan D'Aloia

A fanatical fisherman calls his doctor and says, "Doc, you gotta help me out. It's an emergency. My baby swallowed a fish hook!"

The doctor says, "Bring him to my office. I'll meet you there."

Before the doctor could even get out the door, the phone rings again and the fisherman says, "Never mind, Doc. I found another fish hook."

A hillbilly went on a two-week fishing trip. The entire time he was only able to bag one small trout. When he returned home, he showed the fish to his friend and said, "You know, that one fish cost me around 300 dollars."

"In that case," his friend said, "it's a good thing you didn't catch two."

Trout thrive best in water with a high mineral content, while this is the very sort of water that is used for making Tennessee whiskey. This is why one never finds a trout in a fifth of Jack Daniel's. Or vice versa.

—Milforn Stanley Poltroon

Hook, Line & Stinkers

Q: What do you call a fish with two knees?

A: A two-knee fish

Q: Which fish only comes out at night and terrorizes all the other fish in London?

A: Jack the Kipper

Q: What's the best way to get in the fish business?

A: On a small scale

Q: What is it that swims in the sea, carries a Tommy gun, and makes you an offer you can't refuse?

A: The Codfather

Q: What is full of fish, sits on the bottom of the ocean and shakes?

A: A nervous wreck

Q: How do you stop a fish from smelling?

A: Cut off its nose

Q: Why did the guppy enlist in the motorized division of the Army?

A: So it could be in a fish tank

Q: What fish always wins at poker?

A: The card shark

Q: How do sharks fight?

A: They get into fish-ticuffs.

A fish on the hook is better than ten in the brook.

—Fishing Proverb

There are better fish stories in the sea

than ever came out of it.

—Henny Youngman

A couple of frogs are sitting on a lily pad at the fishing hole. A fly breezes by and one of the frogs snatches it with his tongue. The other frog, looking on, says, "Time sure is fun when you're having flies."

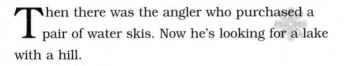

Then there was the angler who purchased a pair of water skis. Now he's looking for a lake with a hill.

Deep in an African jungle, a guy is fishing in the river when he hears a rumbling sound behind him. He turns around and finds himself face to face with an 800-pound lion. Immediately, the fisherman lets go of his pole and drops to his knees in desperate prayer. After a minute or so he happens to catch sight of the lion right beside him, on his knees with paws raised in supplication. Surprised, the fisherman says, "Now see here. I am on my knees praying to my Lord for deliverance. You're only a dumb animal. What could you possibly be doing?"

"Whaddaya think, Bud?" says the lion. "I'm saying grace."

The biggest fish I caught got away.

—Eugene Field

No honest person is a successful fisherman.

—Robert Tomlin

T he answer is debate. And the question?

What is it that lures de fish?

A guy rushes into a fishing supply place and hurriedly says, "I have to catch the ferry and I need some bait, quick!"

The store clerk, with a quizzical look on his face, responds, "I dunno, sir...I don't think we have any bait that a ferry would like."

Two old fishermen, Carmine and Fenster, were out in some rough weather when Carmine suddenly lost his dentures over the side of the boat. Fenster, a sly old codger, decided to play a prank on Carmine. He removed his own false teeth, tied them on his line and made believe he had caught the missing dentures. He pulled the line in, unhooked the dentures and gave them to his friend. Carmine thanked Fenster, slipped the dentures into his mouth, then took them out and said disgustedly, "They're not mine. They don't fit!"

So he threw them back in the water.

Man can learn a lot from fishing. When the fish are biting, no problem in the world is big enough to be remembered.

—Oa Battista

When four fishermen get together,

there's always a fifth.

—Spencer Apollonio

A visitor to a local fishing spot asked one of the anglers, "Is this a good river for fish?"

"I'd say so. I can't persuade any to come out."

The game warden approached the boy who was fishing by the lake. "Hey, son. Can't you read? The sign says 'No Fishing Allowed.'"

The boy whispered, "I'm fishing very quietly, sir."

A Texan visits a friend in Minnesota and they go out fishing one afternoon.

When his friend lands a fairly big one, the Texan says, "That's a nice fish. Can I use it for bait?"

Two guys are out fishing for hours with nary a nibble. Finally, to break the boredom one guy says to the other, "Say, have I ever showed you pictures of my kids?"

The other guy responds, "No, and you can't imagine how much I appreciate it."

"If Today Was A Fish, I'd Throw It Back In"

—Song title

I estimate that there are 45,000 fish in the River Brule, and although I haven't caught them all yet, I've intimidated them.

—President Calvin Coolidge, when asked about his luck while on a fishing excursion

Fenwick has a heart attack and dies while on a fishing trip in Montana. The other members of his fishing party are trying to figure out a sensitive way to break the news to his wife. None of them know Mrs. Fenwick, so they elect the local sheriff to inform her since they assume he's had to do that sort of thing before. The sheriff rings the Fenwicks' doorbell. When a woman answers the door, he asks, "Are you the widow Fenwick?"

She responds, "No, I'm Mrs. Fenwick."

The sheriff says, "No you're not."

HO-HO-HO!

Q: What does Santa call his fishing rod?

A: The North Pole

Gertrude: You don't really believe your husband's story that he spent the whole day fishing, do you? Why, he didn't catch a single fish.

Gloria: That's why I believe him.

Fishing is just like romance...the next best thing to experiencing it is talking about it.

—Anonymous

Fishing, with me, has always been an excuse to drink in the daytime.

—Jimmy Cannon

Then there was the sad, lonely fish...seems that after the ocean fishing ship had come and gone he realized that he, in fact, was the sole survivor.

A Texan was telling his friend about the 20 pound bass he caught. His friend asked, "Was it tough bringing him in?"

"Yeah," drawled the Texan, "but it wasn't nearly as tough as the five pound grasshopper I caught it with."

Two clothing salesmen are on a fishing vacation. One says to the other, "This is really great, but I don't think it can top last year's vacation."

The second clothing salesman asks, "What'd you do last year?"

"I went to Italy," responds the first clothing salesman, "and, believe it or not, I actually met the Pope."

"Wow!" exclaims the second clothing salesman. "What kind of guy is he?"

"Oh, about a 38 medium."

He's just perfect for mounting.

—Mike Hulbert,
pro golfer and avid fisherman,
on the birth of his 8 lb., 3 oz. son

It Was SO Big...

Harry: You wouldn't believe the size of the fish I caught yesterday!

Larry: How big was it?

Harry: It was so big I dislocated my shoulders describing it.

Egbert was talking about the humongous fish he caught.

"How big was it?" asked his friend, Willie.

"It was the biggest I've ever seen."

Willie said, "That doesn't tell me very much. Can you measure it with your hands?"

Egbert looked around the room and responded, "Yeah, but we'll have to go outside."

A fisherman was telling about the big one that got away. With hands outstretched as far as possible he said, "It was at least this big. I never saw such a fish!"

"That I can believe," retorted his friend.

Daughter: Mommy, do all fairy tales start with "Once upon a time?"

Mommy: No, honey. Sometimes they start with "I'm telling you. That fish must have been at least four feet long."

McGee was well known for his fibs when it came to catching the big one. But one day he actually reeled in two giant flounders. He invited a few of his fishing cronies over for dinner to show his big catches. He had a problem, though, on how to serve the fish. He said to his wife, "If I use both fish it'll look like I'm bragging."

Mrs. McGee suggested that he serve a piece of each flounder.

"Nah," said McGee, "if I cut 'em up, they'll never believe I caught two giant flounders."

In a flash, McGee came up with an idea.

That night as his buddies were seated at the table, McGee walked into the dining room with a platter displaying one of the biggest flounders any of them had seen. Suddenly, McGee tripped and fell. At the same time, the fish platter crashed to the floor.

The cunning McGee appeared to be flustered, got up and called out to his wife, "Honey, bring in the other flounder."

Fishing is incessant expectation and perpetual disappointment.

—Arthur Young

Herman: Well, the fishing wasn't so great today.

Thurman: But I thought you said you had thirty bites.

Herman: Yeah, one tiny fish and 29 mosquitoes.

Q: Why can't you trust fishermen and shepherds?

A: Because they live by hook and by crook

Harvey bagged a giant tuna and was lugging it to the cleaning shed when he ran into his friend Howie who was carrying about a dozen small minnows. When Howie spotted him he said, "Hey, Harv...I see you just caught the one, eh?"

Mrs. Jones was trying to teach her second graders the importance of 'patience'. She showed the class a picture of a boy fishing and said, "See, even things that are fun, like fishing, require 'patience'. Why, look at that boy. He's sitting very quietly, waiting. He's very 'patient'. Okay boys and girls, if you were going to go fishing what is the most important thing to have?"

A voice from the back of the class rang out, "Bait!"

It's a crime to catch a fish in some waters,
and a miracle in others.

—Geoff Scowcroft

*Since three-fourths of the earth's surface
is water and one-fourth land, it's perfectly
clear the good Lord intended that man
spend three times as much time fishing as
he does plowing.*

—Anonymous

Q: What's the difference between a man fishing in a kayak and an angler standing along the shoreline?

A: It's row vs. wade.

St. Peter confronts a guy at the Pearly Gates. "Sorry, buddy, but you told one too many lies while you lived on earth. I can't allow you to come in here."

"Aw, St. Peter. Can't you remember when you, too, were a fisherman?"

A couple of fishermen are talking. One says to the other, "I just love this sport. Man against nature. Fisherman versus fish. The fresh air. The solitude. Everything's great. And why do you fish?"

The second guy says, "Because my son's learning the trumpet."

The question of how fast fish grow

depends on who catches them.

—Anonymous

Three pals, Farr, Smith and Away, went deep sea fishing one afternoon but didn't return to port as scheduled.

The Coast Guard snapped into action and organized a search for the trio which went on for days.

Finally, when almost all hope was gone, the rescue planes spotted two of the men clinging to wreckage which had been carried hundreds of miles by the currents. There was no trace of the third fisherman, Away.

A rescue boat was dispatched and after they pulled Smith and Farr out of the water, the Coast Guard heard the pair's eerie tale.

"We were fishing about 20 miles offshore when a strange fog came up out of nowhere," said Farr.

"Yeah, and suddenly the boat began rocking violently," said Smith.

"Then a giant fire-breathing fish with long dorsal spines, purple and orange scales and teeth twelve inches long emerged from the deep and smashed the boat into kindling. We only survived by playing dead."

"Wow!" said the young Coast Guard officer. "That must have been some fish!"

"Oh, that's nothing," said one of the anglers. "You should have seen the one that got Away!"

A newspaper ad salesman calls on Bailey, the bait and tackle shop owner.

"No thanks," says Bailey. "I've been in business 27 years without spending a nickel on advertising."

"Really," says the salesman. "Say...can you tell me what's the name of that church across the street?"

"That's St. Mary's."

"Has it been there long?"

"More than 100 years."

"They still ring the bell, don't they?"

Wouldn't it be great if all guys showed as much patience with their wives as they do with fish?

—Rory Tomlinson

At the altar, I little realized I was pledged
to love, honor, and obey three outboard
motors, the ways of the river, the whims
of the tide, and the wiles of the fish, as
well as Bill, the man of my choice.

—Beatrice Cook

George is lying face down on the road with his ear to the pavement. A stranger comes up to him and says, "Hey, what are you doing?"

George says, "A green pickup truck, two fishermen in it with their poles hanging out back... vanity license plates that say 'Gone Fishing.'"

The stranger says, "You can tell all that just from putting your ear to the ground?"

"No. I'm talking about the truck that ran me over a few minutes ago."

The vessel was going down by the bow and the captain of the sinking charter boat came out on deck and asked the fishermen if anyone knew how to pray.

"Yes...I know how to pray," answered a minister.

"Good," the captain said. "Then start praying, Reverend. The rest of us will put on our life jackets...We're one short."

Q: What happens to fishermen who lie when they die?

A: They lie still.

Fishermen are born honest, but they get over it.

—Ed Zern

In seeing some of the new fishermen on the old riffles, I'm reminded of a friend who told me he's recently taken up golf because he likes the clothes.

—John Merwin

"You know," griped Mrs. Riley to her husbsand, "when you come home from your little fishing trip, I ask you about your day, how they were biting, how many did you catch and so forth. But you never bother to ask me about my day. I've got shopping to do, a house to clean, four kids to watch, washing to do and I never get a word of interest from you."

"Sorry, dear," said Mr. Riley. "How was your day?"

"Don't ask. Just don't ask," complained Mrs. Riley.

Murphy was fishing in Maine even though the season was officially closed. A stranger approached him and said, "Have you caught anything?"

"Have I caught anything?" exclaimed Murphy. "I got a couple hundred pounds of the finest rock bass you ever saw iced down in my trunk."

"Do you know who I am?" asked the stranger.

"No."

"I'm the state game warden. Who are you?"

"I'm the biggest liar in the whole state."

The perfect vacation spot is where the fish bite and the mosquitoes don't.

—Joe Dolan

*If fish landed were as big as stories told
about them, sardines would have to be
packed and sold in garbage cans!*

—Bob Fischbein

Waldo agreed to take his little brother Wally fishing while their parents went shopping.

When the parents came home, Waldo said, "I'll never take Wally fishing again. I didn't get a single bite."

"I'm sure he'll be quiet next time," said his father. "All you have to do is explain to him that noise will scare the fish and they'll swim away."

"It wasn't that," said Waldo. "He ate my bait."

Then there was the aristocratic fish...His ancestors swam under the QE2.

The clergyman was an avid angler. During a wedding ceremony he asked the groom, "Do you promise to love, honor and cherish this woman?"

"I do," the groom replied.

The clergyman turned to the bride and said, "Okay, reel him in!"

"How good's the fishing here?"

"I can't really say. I've been here two weeks and I've dropped 'em a line each day, but so far I haven't gotten a reply."

So many fish. So little time.

—Fishing Proverb

Here's a guy standing in cold water up to his liver throwing the world's most expensive clothesline at trees.

—P.J. O'Rourke, on fly fishing

A guy goes on his annual fishing trip to Minnesota. On the boat he notices the seat next to him is empty so he says to the guy on the other side, "Wow...to have a no-show on a big trip like this."

The other guy says, "That's my wife's seat."

"How come she's not here?" asks the first guy. "Is she sick?"

"No. She's dead."

"Gee, I'm sorry to hear that," says the first guy. "But couldn't you find a friend or relative to take her place?"

"I'm afraid not. They're all at her funeral."

George and Charlie, two fishermen down in the Florida Everglades, were fishing on a small creek when out of a dense thicket of grass charged the biggest, meanest alligator anyone had ever seen.

Standing still in fear, George said to his companion, "He looks hungry. What are we going to do?"

Charlie started backing away and said, "I'm going to run for it."

"Are you crazy?" George asked in a tense whisper. "Gators have been clocked at thirty miles per hour. We'll never outrun him."

"I don't have to outrun him," replied Charlie. "I only have to outrun *you!*"

All things come to those who bait.

—Fishing Proverb

Angus McCorkle, Scotland's most prominent atheist, decided that while most people were wasting their time in church Christmas morning, it'd be a perfect time for him to go fishing.

He set off in a small boat across Loch Ness until he reached the midway point and dropped his line in the water.

Presently there was a great bubbling in the water and the disturbance grew and grew until his tiny boat was lifted high out of the water on the great back of the Loch Ness monster which turned its head, bared its huge teeth and craned its long neck around to reach Angus.

Terrified, Angus cried out, "Oh, God...save me from this terrible beastie!"

From above, a deep voice boomed out, "Angus, I thought you didn't believe in Me."

Angus shouted back, "Come on and work with me a wee bit, Lord. Ten minutes ago, I dinna believe in the Loch Ness monster either!"

HO-HO-HO!

Santa will never forget the time he went fishing in Florida and accidentally dropped his billfold into the water. It no sooner splashed into the spring when a carp swam up and grabbed a corner. As it sank a few inches lower, another carp approached and took another corner and then two more carp appeared and took ahold of the remaining corners. He couldn't believe his eyes! It was the first time he had ever seen carp-to-carp walleting.

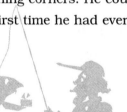

The curious thing about fishing is you never want to go home. If you catch anything, you can't stop. If you don't catch anything, you hate to leave in case something might bite.

—Gladys Taber

No fisherman ever fishes as much as he wants to...this is the first great rule of fishing, and it explains a world of otherwise inexplicable behavior.

—Geoffrey Norman

The widow Abernathy called the newspaper to inquire about the cost of a death notice.

"It's six dollars for six words," the classified clerk answered.

The Abernathys didn't amass their considerable fortune by throwing that kind of money around so the widow said, "Can't I just get two words...'Abernathy's dead'?"

"No, I'm sorry. Six dollars is the minimum...You still have four words left."

Mrs. Abernathy thought for a moment and then added, 'Fishing gear for sale.'

Have you heard about the fishermen who complained to the United Nations that they were being harassed in international waters?

The U.N. promised to mullet over.

Hal and Sal went fishing one Sunday morning, but Hal began to feel guilty.

"I suppose we should have gone to church," said Hal.

Sal responded, "I don't think so. I couldn't have gone to church, anyway. My wife's at home in bed with the flu."

If I were asked to give one word of advice to the angler planning to take his family with him on a fishing holiday, I'd give it...Don't.

—Joe Pisarro

I wonder if (Kevin) Bass is lonely now that Steve Trout is in the American League.

—Atlanta Braves
baseball announcer Skip Caray

A novice fisherman out on a small boat notices another guy on another small boat open up his tackle box and take out a mirror. The novice, out of curiosity, approaches the other guy and asks why he has a mirror.

"That's for catching the fish. I shine the sunlight on the water which makes the fish come up to the top. Then I nab 'em."

"Wow! Hey, I'll give you ten bucks for that mirror," offers the novice.

"Done deal."

The novice buys the mirror, then asks the guy, "By the way, have you caught a lot of fish this week?"

"You're the eighth."

A couple of anglers are boating on a lake at an Indian reservation. All of a sudden, the lake is surrounded by some natives who are more than a bit upset that these guys are fishing on their property. Off in the distance, the fishermen hear the beat of a drum. One of the guys says, "I don't like the sound of those drums."

A moment later, a distant voice yells, "He's not our regular drummer."

Now comes April when intelligent worms go underground because, with the trout season approaching, there is danger of being plucked away from home and loved ones, skewered on a hook and flung into the bitter numbing cold of a mountain brook. This is bad for worms.

—Red Smith

*Any man who can swap horses or catch
fish, and not lie about it, is just about as
pious as men ever get to be in this world.*

—Josh Billings

A California Fisheries Department inspector boarded the ship that had just come in from a deep sea fishing trip in the Pacific.

"I want to inspect your catch," he said to one angler.

"I only caught one fish...this thirteeen pound snapper, but the funny thing is, when I opened him up, I noticed he'd gulped down a two pound blue. And inside that blue was this whiting."

"Give me your name and address," commanded the inspector. "That whiting is undersize."

Q: What is the dumbest fish in the school called?

A: Dinner

The fisherman's credo: If at first you don't succeed...lie.

I get all the truth I need in the newspaper every morning, and every chance I get I go fishing, or swap stories with fishermen, to get the taste of it out of my mouth.

—Ed Zern

It is a silly fish that is caught twice with the same bait.

—Thomas Fuller

Q: What fish get along the best?

A: Sole mates

Dudley's applying for a job at the bait and tackle shop. The owner checks his application and exclaims, "You've been fired from every place you worked!"

Dudley responds, "Yessir, I'm no quitter!"

In the Jersey Pine Barrens, two fishermen were having a high old time sippin' suds and hauling the big ones in one after another. Suddenly, a game warden burst from the bushes and blew his whistle. At once, one of the fishermen dropped his rod and made a break for it. The game warden gave chase as they ran through the briars and brambles. They continued into the pine woods and both were ripped by thorns and picked up chiggers along the way. At long last, the fisherman tripped over a stump and fell to the ground, enabling the game warden to catch up.

"Have you got a fishing license, boy?" the warden breathlessly demanded.

"Certainly, sir," replied the angler. "Right here in my wallet," he said, taking out the card.

"Well, you have got to be the dumbest guy I've ever met," said the warden, shaking his head. "Don't you know you don't have to run away from me when you have a license?"

"Yes, sir," said the fisherman. "But you see, my friend back there...he doesn't have a license."

McDuff is fishing off the north coast of Scotland where the weather is playing havoc with 40-knot winds and unbelievably rough waters. Nonetheless, he's out there and, in no time at all, McDuff has a tremendous bite. The fish is fighting tooth and nail, but McDuff finally lands it. As he does, the fish says, "Please don't hurt me."

McDuff can't believe his ears! It's a talking salmon! McDuff asks, "What's your name?"

"Rusty," replies the salmon.

After a brief conversation, McDuff and Rusty exchange goodbyes and McDuff returns the salmon to the water.

A few years go by before McDuff goes back to the same fishing spot. Again, the weather conditions are poor, there's a driving rain and howling winds. This time, McDuff's not so lucky. He's out there for hours without a bite but just as he's about to call it a day, he gets a big one. He's fighting the fish for almost an hour before he finally brings it in.

The fish says, "Remember me?"

"Oh, my gosh," says McDuff. "Rusty...it's been years. What have you been up to?"

"I've been swimming around the sea and I found this wreck. I was so taken by it that, for the last year and a half, I've written a book about it."

"Oh, really. What's it called?" asks McDuff.

"Titanic Verses by Salmon Rusty."

Q: What did Humphrey Bogart say to the pianist fish?

A: "Play it again, Salmon."

The owner of The Rod & Reel, a fishing gear shop, was griping to a friend about how poorly his business was doing.

"I had that problem once, too," said the friend, "but I solved the dilemma."

"How's that?"

"Simple," said the friend. "The secret is to work only half days."

"Wow! That's incredible!"

"And the best part," the friend continued, "is that it really doesn't matter which twelve hours you work."

All men are equal before a fish.

—President Herbert Hoover

Fish should be cleaned immediately after catching for best flavor and aroma. Fishermen also smell better if they are bathed from time to time.

—Milford Stanley Poltroon

A vacationer was fishing off the coast of Florida when his boat suddenly capsized. Fearful of alligators, he clung to the boat rather than swim to the shore for safety. He noticed another fisherman who was standing along the shore and yelled, "Are there any gators in this water?"

The other fisherman said, "No, they haven't been in these waters for years."

The vacationer, pacified by that comment, began swimming toward shore.

With a considerable distance left to swim, he hollered, "How come there are no gators?"

"The sharks got 'em."